Jessa
Merry Christmas
2005 ♡

THIS JOURNAL BELONGS TO:

_____

I started writing on:

this day _____

in the year _____

in the city of _____

and I was _____ *years old.*

I filled up the last page on:

this day _____

in the year _____

in the city of _____

and I was _____ *years old.*

It was given to me by:

_____

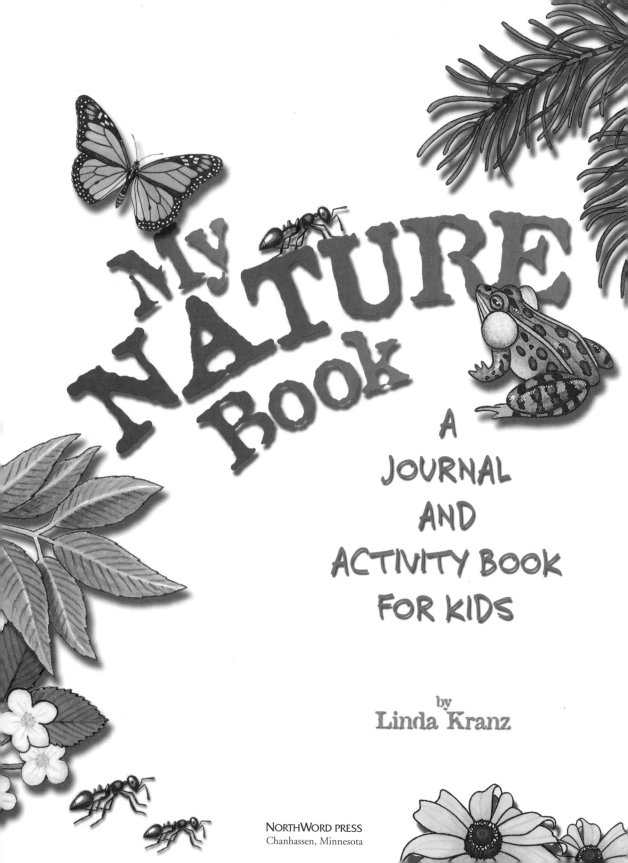

My NATURE Book

A JOURNAL AND ACTIVITY BOOK FOR KIDS

by
Linda Kranz

NORTHWORD PRESS
Chanhassen, Minnesota

Composed in the United States of America
Designed by Lois A. Rainwater
Edited by Aimee Jackson
Illustrations by Linda Garrow and John F. McGee
Digital illustrations composed by Lois A. Rainwater

Books for Young Readers
NorthWord Press
18705 Lake Drive East
Chanhassen, MN 55317
www.northwordpress.com

ISBN 1-55971-893-5

Printed in China
10 9 8 7 6 5 4 3 2 1

A thank you

to those who had the foresight

to set aside land

for national parks, national monuments,

state parks, city parks,

and wilderness areas, so that

all of us can enjoy

our time outdoors.

—L. K.

A NOTE FROM THE AUTHOR

Our family was out hiking one weekend not long ago when we spotted a mother hummingbird and her tiny nest—what a rare sight! We watched her sitting there silent and motionless. Not wanting to disturb her, we continued our trek upstream. That afternoon we also saw a very long, sleek gopher snake; a tall great blue heron; and a turtle sunning himself on a fallen branch in the creek. Sometimes when we're out hiking, we don't see a single animal. Then there are days like this that are exciting and fun to talk about with family and friends.

We have seen black bears, foxes, horned toads, raccoons, snakes, skunks, lizards, deer, coyotes, elk, tarantulas, and rabbits. Each encounter has its own story. We have captured some on film, but most

sightings I have only written about in my journals.

Here's a journal entry I wrote several years ago as we were about to head back home after our annual trip to the mountains:

" *The cabin was cozy. Four windows with curtains that tied back in the day and fell shut for privacy at night. A comfortable place where we could kick back and relax. Mostly it was a dry place to sleep because late in the summer we always seem to encounter daily afternoon or nighttime thunderstorms. We spent our days out in the forest by rivers and streams, watching clouds build above the pine-covered canyons. Reading, fishing, carving wood to float tiny boats downstream, skipping rocks across the calm part of the*

river, watching butterflies, searching for four-leaf clovers, or drawing the landscape around us.

Then before we'd know it, the days would be almost over. We always planned it so that we would have a good vantage point to watch the colorful sunset and then we would head back as the stars were coming out. In the evening, the cabin was a place where conversations were plentiful and laughter filled the small spaces inside. After dinner there were board games and stories.

During the night, thunderstorms would often sneak into the valley and the metal roof on the cabin really had a way of accentuating the sound of the rain pouring down. A few times we couldn't even hear ourselves talk it was so loud. We would watch the electric

show out our windows and feel the ground shake beneath us. Soon, the storm moved on and we were able to fall asleep so we would be rested for another day outdoors. "

I love rereading the adventures we've had over the years as we explored different places. I'm glad we have the journals and photographs to remind us of these very special times.

And now you can capture your memories from nature inside this journal!

TIPS FOR JOURNAL WRITERS

This is your journal—a place for you to write about and illustrate the experiences that are uniquely your own. We all view the world in our own ways. Journaling is sometimes even better than photographs for helping us to remember a time or place because we can describe not only the sights, but also the sounds and smells, and most importantly, how we were feeling at the time. Someday you may want to go back and reread your journal, and the more descriptive your entries are, the more they will help you to remember those days gone by.

Always date your pages and write in the day of the week. Journaling captures a time that will never be the same again.

You will notice that I have included lots of "thought starters" to get your ideas flowing. There are also many blank pages where you can write down your own experiences, or draw anything you want. This journal can easily slip into your backpack so that you can write notes or draw pictures while you are relaxing on the hiking trail. Or you can write or draw on the ride back, or perhaps you will want to wait until you are at home in your own room just before bedtime. Whichever you choose, be sure to set aside time to record your thoughts while your memory is still fresh and these pages will fill up easily.

So, what are you waiting for? Grab your journal and go out and explore!

—LINDA KRANZ

Find a comfortable spot. Close your eyes and sit very still. Listen for the sounds all around you.

What do you hear?

How does the air smell?

What is the temperature like?

Now, open your eyes.

Continue to sit very still.

Notice the movement around you.

What do you see?

Write about what you discover.

If you could **invent something** that would be very useful or that would be beneficial to someone **who spends a lot of time outdoors,** what would it be? Describe it here.

TRAVEL NOTES!

DATE: _____ DAY OF THE WEEK: _____

TIME WE LEFT: _____ WHEN WE RETURNED: _____

TODAY WE DROVE TO: _____

WHY WE WANTED TO VISIT THIS PLACE: / HOW WE HEARD ABOUT IT:
_____
_____

WE'VE BEEN HERE BEFORE: / THIS IS OUR FIRST TIME HERE:
_____
_____

WHAT THE WEATHER WAS LIKE:
_____
_____

INTERESTING THINGS THAT WE SAW:
_____
_____

HOW WE SPENT THE DAY:
_____
_____

SOUVENIRS WE BROUGHT HOME:
_____
_____

NEXT TIME WE GO BACK TO THIS PLACE, I WANT TO:
_____
_____

WHAT I WILL REMEMBER MOST ABOUT THIS DAY:
_____
_____

DRAW

Draw whatever you want on these pages.

Let your imagination go WILD!

DRAW

Write about something **YOU DISCOVERED** that you never noticed before.

_____

_____

_____

_____

_____

_____

_____

_____

_____

_____

_____

_____

_____

_____

_____

Like how the wings of a dragonfly sparkle in the sunlight, or how the song of one bird is so different from another. Or how wind sways the branches of a tree from side to side or in circles.

DRAW

"I
am
inclined
to
think
that
the
flowers
we
most
love
are
those
we
knew
when
we
were
very
young."

--Dorothy Thompson

Sleeping birds do not fall off branches because...

...they have a way of "locking" their feet around a perch. **There is a tendon in the birds' feet** that automatically locks them in place.

What type of **WEATHER EXTREMES** have you experienced?

The hottest temperature?

The coldest?

The most rain?

The most snow?

A HAIL-STORM?

The driest summer?

A drought?

LIGHTNING that was too close for comfort?

Describe your experiences.

A FUN PROJECT FOR YOU!

Make Banana Bread or Muffins to Take with You on Hiking Trips

This is a great snack to take along to eat on your hike, or on the ride home.

Ingredients:

- ❄ 2 ¼ cups (315 g) sifted flour
- ❄ ¾ teaspoon (2.75 g/3.7 ml) baking soda
- ❄ ⅛ teaspoon (.75 g/.6 ml) salt
- ❄ ¼ cup (½ stick/55 g) butter, at room temperature
- ❄ ¾ cup (150 g) sugar
- ❄ 2 eggs
- ❄ 2 medium-size ripe bananas, mashed (about ¾ cup/1.8 dl)
- ❄ ½ cup (1.2 dl/115 g) sour cream

Optional (choose one):

- ❄ ½ cup (55 g) chopped walnuts or pecans, or
- ❄ ½ cup (60 g) dried cranberries, or
- ❄ ½ cup (85 g) chocolate chips

Preheat oven to 350°F (175°C). Butter and flour a loaf pan, or spray with cooking spray. Sift together flour, baking soda, and salt. In a large bowl, cream butter and sugar until light and fluffy. Beat in eggs. Add sifted dry ingredients, alternating with banana and sour cream. Mix until just blended. Blend in nuts, cranberries, or chocolate chips if using and pour into loaf pan. Bake one hour or until toothpick inserted in center comes out clean. Remove from oven and let cool. Slice and wrap in plastic wrap or place in a resealable plastic bag. Freeze. The bread will be ready for your next outing. If you don't have a cooler, you can take the frozen slices with you and by the time you're ready to eat the bread, it will be thawed. You could also make muffins with the recipe to freeze and take with you (wrap them individually in plastic wrap).

ABOUT MY PROJECT!

How did my Banana BREAD taste?

Did other people enjoy it?

Will I make it again? If so, would I change anything about the recipe?

DRAW

Do you

remember

the

brightest

rainbow

you have

ever seen?

Draw it,

or put a

photo here.

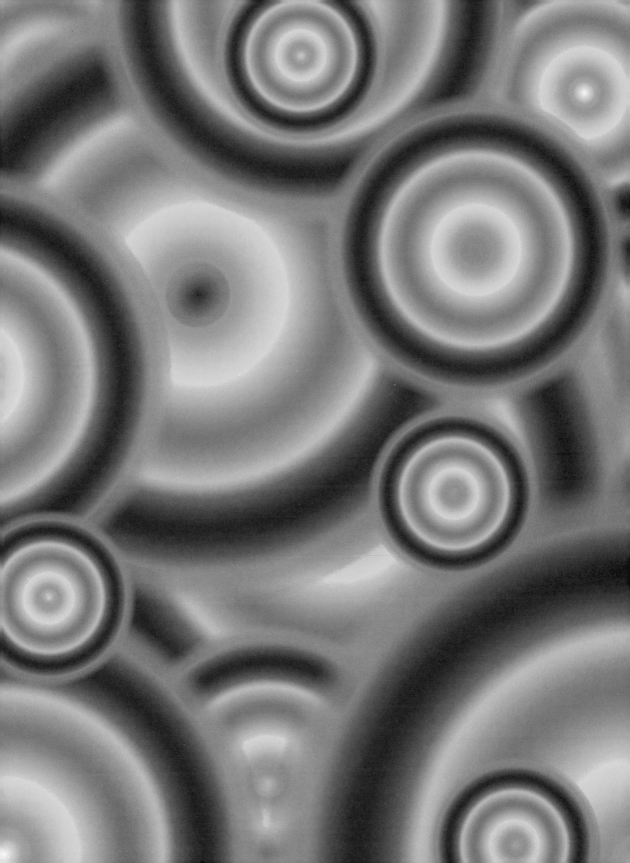

Do you think there are animals out there in the world somewhere that have never been seen by a human? If so, what do you think they look like? And what would you name them?

Draw

what

you

think

those

animals

would

look

like

on

this

page.

Do

they

look

like

the

names

you

gave

them?

On a nice day when there are plenty of puffy white clouds in the sky, lie on your back in a patch of green grass. Make shapes out of the clouds. Draw some of the shapes you see.

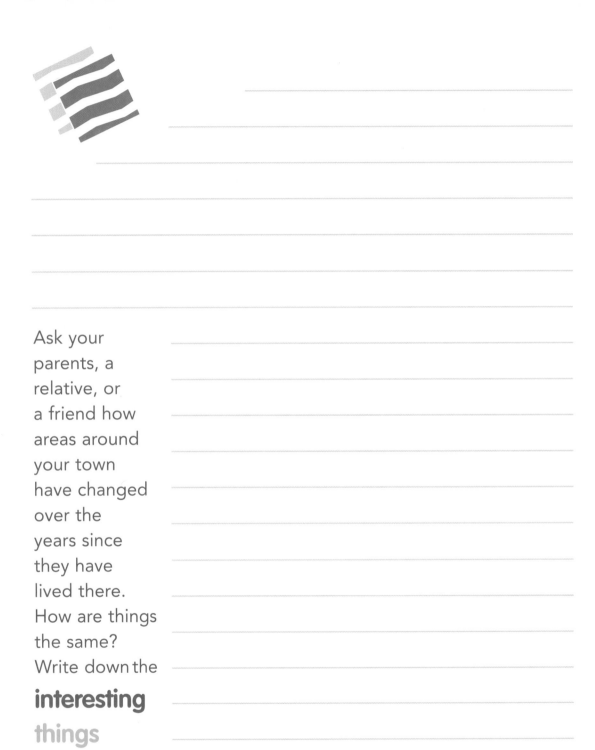

Ask your parents, a relative, or a friend how areas around your town have changed over the years since they have lived there. How are things the same? Write down the **interesting** things **that you** learn.

You could learn more about how YOUR TOWN has changed by going to a MUSEUM or visiting your Chamber of Commerce.

A FUN PROJECT FOR YOU!

Make Luminarias
[loom-uh-NAR-ee-uhs]

You will need:

* ❄ medium to large clean and dry empty metal soup can or coffee can (try to find a can that is smooth on the sides)
* ❄ hammer
* ❄ nail
* ❄ small votive candle
* ❄ permanent marker

Draw a design on the outside of your can using the permanent marker. A star, a tree, a snowman, letters or numbers, or any shape you want. (You could also draw a pattern on paper first, cut it out, and trace around it onto the can.) Fill the can with water. Freeze it. Make sure it is frozen solid when you begin your project.

Lay the frozen can on a thick towel to help stabilize it, and to give you a better working surface. With the help of an adult, use the nail to hammer holes along the lines of your design. Pound the holes all the way through the sides of the can. Find a place to leave your can while the ice melts, or set the can in warm water to melt the ice more quickly. When the ice has melted, dry your can completely. Be careful! The edges of the holes inside the can will be very sharp. Carefully place the candle inside. Put your can outside where it can be seen by passers-by. Wait for sunset and ask an adult to light the candle for you. You could make several luminarias and they could light the way to your front door!

ABOUT MY PROJECT!

What shapes did I design for my cans?

Did my neighbors tell me how beautiful they were?

Will I make it again? If so, what will I do differently?

DRAW

If you could
Draw The Wind,
what would it look like?

Are you a good traveler?

Why or why not?

What do you like or dislike about
waking up in a new place?

If you could spend
a week anywhere that
you choose, where
would it be and what
would you like to do there?

TRAVEL NOTES!

DATE: _____   DAY OF THE WEEK: _____

TIME WE LEFT: _____   WHEN WE RETURNED: _____

TODAY WE DROVE TO: _____

WHY WE WANTED TO VISIT THIS PLACE: / HOW WE HEARD ABOUT IT: _____

_____

WE'VE BEEN HERE BEFORE: / THIS IS OUR FIRST TIME HERE: _____

_____

WHAT THE WEATHER WAS LIKE: _____

_____

INTERESTING THINGS THAT WE SAW: _____

_____

HOW WE SPENT THE DAY: _____

_____

SOUVENIRS WE BROUGHT HOME: _____

_____

NEXT TIME WE GO BACK TO THIS PLACE, I WANT TO: _____

_____

WHAT I WILL REMEMBER MOST ABOUT THIS DAY: _____

_____

What would you like to learn more about
when it comes to the subject of nature?

_____

_____

_____

_____

_____

_____

_____

_____

_____

_____

_____

_____

_____

_____

_____

_____

_____

_____

_____

_____

DRAW

"The Earth laughs in flowers."

--Ralph Waldo Emerson

"The smell of the rain is rich with life."

--Estela Portillo Trambley

A FUN PROJECT FOR YOU!

Take a Nature Walk

Take a walk around your neighborhood.
Write about what you see. Check off any animals,
insects, or reptiles that you might have seen along the way:

SNAKE ☐   LIZARD ☐   SQUIRREL ☐

FROG ☐   SKUNK ☐   SPIDER ☐

CHIPMUNK ☐   ARMADILLO ☐   CRICKET ☐

LADYBUG ☐   DRAGONFLY ☐   BIRD ☐

_____ ☐   _____ ☐   _____ ☐

ABOUT MY PROJECT!

Where did I GO ON MY Nature Walk?

How many items did I check off the list?

Where would I like to go NEXT time?

Good times are for remembering.
Write about GOOD TIMES you've had
in nature that you will NEVER forget.

Have you ever seen something that made you sad when you were out exploring? What was it? Did you talk about it with your parents or an adult?

There are around 400 national parks in this country. Have you ever visited a national park? A state park? If so, which ones? What did you find interesting?

Squirrel, coyote, deer . . . have you ever thought about the names of animals? They were named long ago.

If you could rename them, what would you call them? Or, would you leave them as they are?

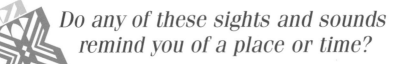

Do any of these sights and sounds remind you of a place or time?

The sound
of a cricket
chirping?

The sound
of waves
lapping against
the shore?

The feel
of warm
sand between
your toes?

The rumbling
of thunder off
in the distance?

Flashes of
lightning in
the sky?

Leaves
changing
as the
temperature
cools?

ANIMAL SIGHTINGS!
WHERE WERE YOU?
WHAT ANIMALS DID YOU SEE THERE?

DATE: _____ PLACE: _____

THE ANIMALS I SAW: _____

_____

_____

_____

DATE: _____ PLACE: _____

THE ANIMALS I SAW: _____

_____

_____

_____

DATE: _____ PLACE: _____

THE ANIMALS I SAW: _____

_____

_____

_____

_____

A FUN PROJECT FOR YOU!

Press Beautiful Flowers or Leaves

You will need:

- ❄ 2 pieces of paper
- ❄ several fresh flowers or leaves
- ❄ some heavy books (like telephone directories)

Place flowers or leaves on one sheet of paper. Separate the petals of the flowers so they look natural. Arrange the flowers and leaves so they won't touch each other. Place the second piece of paper on top of the flowers or leaves. Next, place a heavy book or two on top of the paper. Leave them for a few days, or as long as a week. Your pressed flowers should last for a long time. You can use them to make crafts with, or just enjoy them as they are.

ABOUT MY PROJECT!

Are my FLOWERS and leaves BEAUTIFUL ?

What type of FLOWERS or leaves did I press?

Will I do it again? If so, would I do anything differently?

I wanted to write this down, so I wouldn't forget.

According to a popular myth, raccoons "wash" everything they eat. But this behavior is not related to cleanliness. It's believed to be related to their natural habit of finding food in water.

DRAW

Draw whatever you want here.

Explore places around your neighborhood.

Be a **tourist** in your own town. Often, **beautiful places** are overlooked close to home. Look on a map for **new places** to discover with your **family.** Write about what you **discover.**

What is the most amazing sight that you've seen on your travels? A mountain range? A waterfall? A vast desert? An interesting animal? What made it so striking?

Have you ever heard that lightning never strikes the same place twice?

I
T
i
S
A
m
y
T

The Empire State Building in New York City is struck 20 to 30 times each year.

If you were
given a canoe,
camping gear,
and food for a
week, and you
could choose
one person to
go along with
you on the trip,
who would
you choose to
go with you
and where
would you go?
What do you
think your
adventure
would be
like? Describe
your dream
getaway.

Camouflage is a natural way for animals, reptiles, and insects to blend in with their surroundings. Have you ever been surprised by an insect or animal when you have been out exploring? Be aware next time and write down a few of the things that you discovered.

Many people consider DANDELIONS to be a **nuisance**, yet **butterflies** think they are IRRESISTIBLE.

Make a Rock or Seashell Collection Display

You will need:

❄ cleaned rocks or seashells
❄ a clear glass or plastic container
  (like a flower vase or clean jar)

Carefully place dry, clean rocks or shells in the container, layering them as you go along to create different color, shape, and pattern effects. This is a great way to have your collection in one place. Now display your collection for all to see!

ABOUT MY PROJECT!

How did my display turn out?

What did I learn?

Will I make another one? If so, what will I do differently?

What are
ten things
that you
enjoy
about being
in nature?
Keep adding
to this list.

1

2

3

4

5

6

7

8

9

10

Fireflies, or lightning bugs, are found throughout the tropical and temperate regions of the world. In the United States they live mostly east of the Mississippi River. One reason fireflies glow is to attract mates. Another reason is to avoid predators. Fireflies are filled with a nasty-tasting chemical called lucibufagens that predators don't like. Yet that doesn't stop some predators from eating them. Frogs have been known to devour large numbers of fireflies until they also begin to glow. Draw your own fireflies on this page.

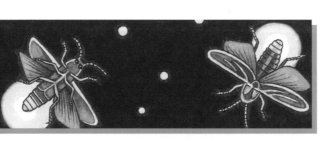

WRITE MORE THOUGHTS ON THIS PAGE
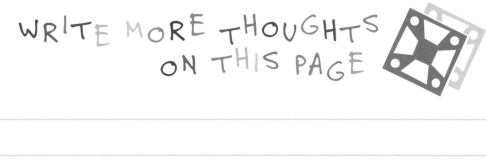

FINISH one of these
THOUGHT STARTERS...

TODAY I DISCOVERED . . . / IN A PERFECT WORLD . . .

HUMMINGBIRDS lay THE SMALLEST eggs OF ANY TYPE of bird.

Their eggs
are less than
one-half
inch long--

HALF the
size of a
jelly bean!

On average,
hummingbirds
consume half
their weight
in sugar
each day.

S P R I N G

*F*ind a tree in your yard, your neighborhood, or at your.........

tree as the seasons change.........

S U M M E R

FALL

.........school that you can watch for a year. Pay attention to the

.........Draw how the tree looks each season.

Winter

How
does
the
night
sky
in your
town
or city
compare
to the
sky
in the
wilderness?

Write about a few of the "**FIRSTS**" in your life.

The
first
time
you
caught
a
fish

The
first
time
you
went
hiking

The

first

time

you

swam

in a

lake

The

first

time

you

climbed

a tree

If you could write your own rules about the natural world, what would they be? Why would your rules be helpful and important?

When you are hiking or camping, pack out everything that you pack in.

When you are hiking or camping, be sure to bring a small trash bag with you so you can leave the natural place that you visit just as you found it. Did you know that certain items take a long time to biodegrade? For instance:

Paper	2-5 months
Orange peels	6 months
Plastic bags	10-20 years
Tin cans	50-100 years
Aluminum cans	80-100 years
Glass bottles	1 million years
Plastic bottles	Never

DRAW

Draw whatever you want on these pages.
Let your imagination SOAR!

"Few forms
of life are
so engaging
as birds."

--Ellen Glasgow

Ask your family what they like most about being in nature. They might teach you something that you've never thought about.

A FUN PROJECT FOR YOU!

Make a Nature Box

You will need:

❄ an empty box with a lid,
   like an old shoe box

Use your box to store things that you find in
nature, like fallen leaves or pinecones, pressed leaves or flowers, rocks, seashells,
feathers, bones, etc. Remember not to keep live insects or animals in your box!
Whenever you open your nature box, it will remind you of a special memory.

ABOUT MY PROJECT!

What did I put in my NATURE BOX?

_____

_____

_____

How long did it take me to find ALL MY TREASURES?

_____

_____

_____

_____

_____

_____

_____

_____

When I look inside my nature box, these memories come to mind...

_____

_____

_____

_____

Butterflies go through four stages of life.
An adult butterfly lays an egg. The egg hatches into a caterpillar larva.
The caterpillar forms the chrysalis. The chrysalis matures into a butterfly.

Preserve Pretty Tree Leaves

Look for newly fallen leaves and small branches on the ground. Gather the leaves you like and take them home for a fun project.

You will need:

- ❄ freshly fallen leaves of various shapes, sizes, and colors
- ❄ small, fallen branches
- ❄ a small bottle of glycerin (you can find it at your local drugstore in the skin-care section or the first-aid section)
- ❄ newsprint to protect your work surface

Spread out several layers of newsprint. Stir together in a jar one part glycerin and three parts hot water. Clip the ends of the leaves and branches a tiny bit so the liquid will be drawn up inside them. Place leaf stems and branches in the mixture and leave for about a week. Make sure only the stems touch the solution (if the leaves touch the solution, they will turn black). Your leaves should retain their appearance and stay beautiful for many years.

ABOUT MY PROJECT!

How did my leaves turn out?

Where will I display them?

Will I keep them, or give them as a gift?

"A good writer
is basically a
storyteller, not
a scholar or
a redeemer of
mankind."

--Isaac Bashevis Singer

Write about a few nature books that you have read that have held your interest.

_____

WHAT DID YOU LIKE BEST ABOUT THEM?

_____
_____
_____
_____
_____
_____
_____
_____

WHAT DID YOU LEARN WHEN YOU READ THEM?

_____
_____
_____
_____
_____
_____
_____
_____

Perhaps one day
you could become an expert on a subject
and write your own book.

DRAW

Look for unusual or surprising things in Nature the next time you are out hiking—like a tree root curled around a rock or a cactus pad shaped like a heart.

DRAW

Draw some
of those
unique
things
here.
Add to these
sketches
over time
as you
find more
unique
things.
Remember
to date your
drawings.

How would you describe the forest, the desert, the prairie, the ocean, or any of your favorite landscapes to someone who has never seen them?

_____

_____

_____

_____

_____

_____

_____

_____

_____

_____

_____

_____

_____

_____

_____

_____

_____

_____

_____

_____

_____

If you want to learn more about DIFFERENT PLACES, go to the LIBRARY, or check it out on the INTERNET.

Write whatever you want here.

If you could talk to someone in another
country about the kinds of wildlife
there, who would you want to talk to?
What would you ask them?

Which EXPLORERS do you ADMIRE?

Lewis and Clark discovered a route to the West Coast. John Wesley Powell mapped the Colorado River. If you could be written about in history books for something that you did, what would you want to be known for? What do you think it would be like to be the very first person to discover a place?

If you could go back in time or go into the future, where would you go and what would you want to learn?

DRAW

Draw the most colorful sunset you have ever seen.

At the bottom of the page, write the date and place where you saw it.

Do you have a **FAVORITE PLACE**
in nature where you like to go?

Why do you like it so much?

_____

_____

_____

_____

How long does it take you to get there?

_____

_____

_____

_____

_____

What do you like to do there?

_____

_____

_____

_____

_____

Describe what the area looks like.

_____

_____

Has something someone said or SOMETHING YOU READ made an impression on how you view the natural world?

Perhaps

a guest speaker

at school?

A show

on **television?**

An article

in a

magazine?

Or a book

that you **read?**

A FUN PROJECT FOR YOU!

Make Delicious Energy-Boosting Trail Mix

Here's a recipe that will help you keep your energy up while you are out hiking.

Ingredients:

In a large bowl mix ⅓ cup (80 ml) each of the following ingredients:

- ❄ dried cranberries
- ❄ raisins
- ❄ stick or mini pretzels
- ❄ Multi-Bran Chex cereal
- ❄ Cheerios cereal
- ❄ sunflower seeds
- ❄ unsalted nuts
      (peanuts, pecans, almonds, cashews, etc.)
- ❄ dried banana chips
- ❄ If it's not too hot outside, you could also
      add mini chocolate chips or M&Ms.

Store your trail mix in a resealable plastic bag, or in an airtight container.

ABOUT MY PROJECT!

Was my Trail Mix TASTY?

Did other people enjoy it?

Will I make it again? Would I change anything about the recipe?

DRAW

Follow the path. Notice certain landmarks as you pass them so you can find your way back easily. Some say the way there seems longer than the way back. Do you think this is true?

while hiking, stay put. Carry a whistle. Blow it from time to time. Remember to stay put. • Be alert. If you get bitten or stung by a snake, bee, or other insect or animal, stay calm. Tell an adult. Seek immediate medical attention. • Pay attention when you are hiking.

TRAVEL NOTES!

DATE: _____   DAY OF THE WEEK: _____

TIME WE LEFT: _____   WHEN WE RETURNED: _____

TODAY WE DROVE TO: _____

WHY WE WANTED TO VISIT THIS PLACE: / HOW WE HEARD ABOUT IT: _____

WE'VE BEEN HERE BEFORE: / THIS IS OUR FIRST TIME HERE: _____

WHAT THE WEATHER WAS LIKE: _____

INTERESTING THINGS THAT WE SAW: _____

HOW WE SPENT THE DAY: _____

SOUVENIRS WE BROUGHT HOME: _____

NEXT TIME WE GO BACK TO THIS PLACE, I WANT TO: _____

WHAT I WILL REMEMBER MOST ABOUT THIS DAY: _____

Ladybugs or lady beetles are a very beneficial
group of insects. A single ladybug may consume
as many as 5,000 aphids in its lifetime.
Aphids are tiny insects that suck the juices
from plants, weakening their leaves and stems.

When you are out for a walk, collect leaves
of different sizes and shapes. Trace their patterns
and color them in with colored pencils or crayons.

A FUN PROJECT FOR YOU!

Make a Water Window to Look in a Creek, Stream, River, or Lake

You will need:

- ❄ large metal can
- ❄ large clear plastic bag
- ❄ large rubber band

Remove the top and bottom of the metal can. Place the plastic bag over one end of the can. Secure the bag with a large rubber band. Trim bag if necessary. Place the plastic bag-covered end of the can in the water and look through the open end. Now you can see down into the water!

Or, you can also make the water window using the following instead:

- ❄ ½ gallon (2 l) square milk carton
- ❄ heavy plastic wrap
- ❄ large rubber band
- ❄ masking tape or electrical tape

Cut the top and bottom off the carton. Wrap plastic wrap up and over the sides of one end. Tape plastic wrap securely. Place rubber band on the bottom half of the carton to keep the wrap tight and secure.

ABOUT MY PROJECT!

How did my water window turn out?

_____

_____

_____

_____

What did I learn?

_____

_____

_____

_____

_____

Will I make another one? If so, what will I do differently?

_____

_____

_____

_____

_____

_____

_____

_____

DID YOU KNOW that PINECONES can PREDICT the WEATHER?

Pinecones close when the weather is wet, **and open when it's dry.**

Has the weather ever caused you to CHANGE YOUR PLANS? When? How did it turn out? Describe the worst thing about it and the BEST THING about it.

_____
_____
_____
_____
_____
_____
_____
_____
_____
_____
_____
_____
_____
_____
_____
_____
_____
_____

Star watching is fun. Take time to look up at the night sky. Can you find any constellations? If you watch long enough, you might even see a falling star. Draw a picture of a falling star or a constellation.

Pay attention to the sounds you hear as you wake up each morning.

How early do you hear the birds start to sing? What other sounds do you hear as you lie still and listen?

Have you ever been **camping** or been to a SUMMER CAMP? What was it like? If *you haven't,* would you **like to try** camping sometime? WHAT DO YOU THINK it would be like?

F
A
L
L

Winter

SPRING

SUMMER

What do you notice as each season changes? What is your favorite season of the year? Why? What's the weather like on your birthday? How does it change from year to year?

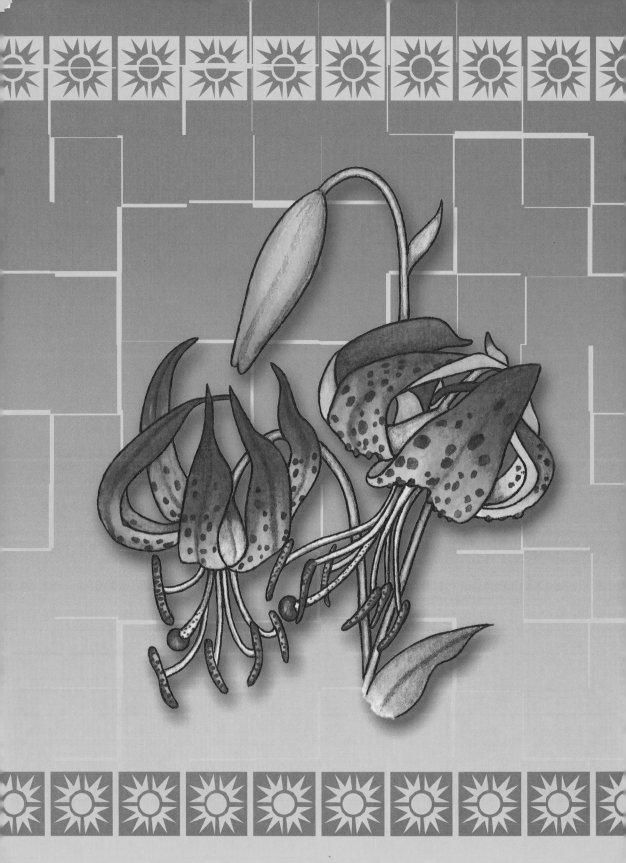

DRAW

"Nature
is
painting
for
us,
day
after
day,
pictures
of
infinite
beauty
if
we
only
have
the
eyes
to
see
them."

--John Ruskin

Write whatever you want on this page.
Let your imagination go WILD!

TRAVEL CHECKLIST!

WHERE ARE WE GOING? _____

_____

WATER BOTTLE ☐	SUNSCREEN ☐	INSECT REPELLENT ☐
FIRST-AID KIT ☐	HAT ☐	COMFORTABLE SHOES ☐
RAIN GEAR ☐	THERMOS ☐	SNACKS ☐
BINOCULARS ☐	CAMERA ☐	EXTRA FILM ☐
LIGHT JACKET ☐	TRASH BAG ☐	NOTEBOOK/PENCILS ☐
WHISTLE ☐	MAGNIFYING GLASS ☐	FLASHLIGHT/BATTERIES ☐

ADD YOUR OWN LIST OF THINGS YOU MIGHT NEED:

_____

_____

_____

_____

_____

_____

_____

_____

_____

The trees that lose their leaves are called deciduous.

Evergreens keep their leaves year-round.

Draw your favorite type of tree, or place a photo here.

Sometimes a song will bring back a memory. When you hear a certain song on the radio, does it remind you of a special place that you have visited?

What is the song?

Where is the special place?

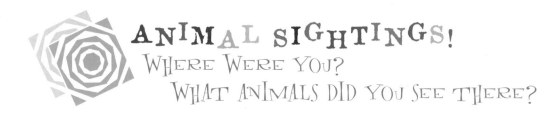

ANIMAL SIGHTINGS!
WHERE WERE YOU?
WHAT ANIMALS DID YOU SEE THERE?

DATE: PLACE:

THE ANIMALS I SAW:

DATE: PLACE:

THE ANIMALS I SAW:

DATE: PLACE:

THE ANIMALS I SAW:

It is
estimated
that
there are
20,000
different
species
of ants.
For this
reason, ants
have been
called
**Earth's
most
successful
species.**
They can
be found
**almost
anywhere**
on the
planet.

Look back through this journal and write about what you feel when you read your entries and look at your drawings. What makes your finished journal special?

LINDA KRANZ is the author of seven journals
and the craft book *Let's Rock! Rock Painting for Kids.*

Linda Kranz would love to hear about one of your
favorite, true-life adventure, wildlife, camping, or getaway stories,
or to hear any suggestions you may have for a future journal.

You can write to her at:
Linda Kranz
P.O. Box 2404
Flagstaff, AZ 86003-2404